THE ARDENNES REMEMBERED

The
ARDENNES
REMEMBERED

THE STORY OF AN
AMERICAN SOLDIER IN WWII

Craig A. Schoeller & Brian Herrmann

Kilroy Publishing

The Ardennes Remembered

Paperback: 978-1-7373213-0-9
Ebook: 978-1-7373213-1-6

Cover Design and Typesetting
Stewart A. Williams | stewartwilliamsdesign.com

Kilroy Publishing

To my grandfather, Craig A. Schoeller.

May you look with pride on this final product and, even though you are gone, may your stories continue to live.

CRAIG A. SCHOELLER

We walk a little slower these days, and the spring in our step is, for the most part, gone. Sometimes you have to speak louder when talking to us. Time has taken, and is taking, its toll on us. Our ranks grow thinner each day.

We probably appear to you like any ordinary group of old people, mostly retirees now, sitting on porch swings or in rocking chairs or wandering around malls. We're ordinary parents and grandparents in all respects save one...

Anonymous

Acknowledgments

Although this book was put together by my grandfather and me over many years, it would have never been realized without the help of others.

I owe a debt of gratitude to those who listened to and attended my grandfather's lectures over the years, not only for their attention and interest in his war experience, but also for their crucial role in helping to preserve his memories by giving him reason to share them. Thank you as well to Vanessa Peters, Milo Brooking, Elisa Bordon Perez, Emiliana Russo, and Hannah Houtz for their comments and suggestions on various drafts.

A special thanks is due to Meg Garnett, Special Collections Librarian at Susquehanna University. I was fortunate enough to have met Meg in the depths of the Blough-Weis Library during the final year of my undergraduate studies. Meg, who possesses a remarkable ability to uncover and compile sources, assisted significantly with research, proofreading, editing, and her much-needed honesty. Her contributions greatly shaped this final draft.

Dr. Martina Kolb, Associate Professor of German Studies at Susquehanna University, also deserves a special thanks for her significant contributions to this work. Martina acted as my advisor throughout my undergraduate studies and has since become a friend. The quality of this book was greatly enhanced by her input. She proofread this piece on multiple occasions and offered valuable criticism. From the beginning, she has been a source of encouragement and guidance not only for this project but throughout my undergraduate studies and beyond. Her suggestions and feedback were invaluable in the creation of this book.

Lastly, none of this could have been possible without our family, whose love and support have been boundless from the start.

Brian Herrmann

A Note on the Ardennes

Every December, when the temperature drops and the cold wind blows and the snow falls on the pine and the spruce, my thoughts go back to 1944 in the Ardennes.

The Ardennes is a woody, hilly region stretching across northeastern France, northern Luxembourg, and eastern Belgium. Four times in modern history it was a pathway for German invasion. During the Franco-Prussian War, Bismarck's troops came through that area. In 1914, it was the Kaiser's turn. In 1940, Hitler's Blitzkrieg hit the region. The Germans bypassed the Maginot Line, came through the Ardennes, and hit France and the low countries. Then, on December 16, 1944, Hitler, in a last desperate move to win the war in the West, struck the same area. His troops crashed right through the line and his intention was to sever the Allied forces and reach Antwerp, Brussels, and Liège. Those German armies hit depleted divisions, green troops, and at first there was panic and confusion.

I know many of you people here remember those times. American troops retreated, and it looked like the Germans were going to make considerable headway. But then brave troops from here and there stemmed the advance. Engineers blew up supply depots and critical bridges. Roadblocks were established. They were trying to reach the Meuse River, but they didn't quite get that far. The Ninth Army and the British forces came down from the north. Patton brought his army up from the Saar to the southern flank and the German offensive was stymied. However, the battle continued for another thirty days and became the largest battle fought by the U.S. Army. We had almost ninety thousand casualties. The Germans had over a hundred thousand, and this battle was fought under winter conditions of the severest nature.

Craig A. Schoeller (in a lecture to his peers)

Preface

I wrote this book with my grandfather Craig A. Schoeller about his experience in a war in which the death toll may well have reached sixty million. During World War II, he was a Private First-Class in Company F, 320th Infantry Regiment, 35th Infantry Division of the United States Army, whose engagements included the Battle of the Bulge. He was captured and held at Stalag XI-B, a German prison camp. After being liberated, he returned to the United States and completed his service in New Jersey, attaining the rank of Staff Sergeant. In the latter years of his life, he shared his experience publicly, often with various veterans' groups. Some of the organizations in which he was active included the Old Baldy and Union League Library Civil War Round Tables, the World War II Lecture Institute, the Rotary Club of Cheltenham-Rockledge, Disabled American Veterans, the American Ex-Prisoner of War Organization, the 35th Division Association, and the Battle of the Bulge Association. On the fiftieth anniversary of D-Day in 1994, he returned to Europe to tour battle locations with other WWII veterans.

I have always been fascinated by my grandfather's war experiences. When I was seven, I asked my grandfather to write out the many war stories he had told me, which then became seven chapters, each a page in length, tucked into a blue fastener folder. It includes pictures of him and the war as well as a hand-drawn map he made outlining his route across Europe (see Appendix A). The cover reads "A Soldier's Story" and features a photograph of him in uniform. Later, I asked him if we could create another version highlighting the more humorous aspects of his experience. This resulted in six brief chapters entitled "Memories: Funny Things That Happened in the Army." Over the years, however, I wondered whether there was still more to his story and whether it could be shared with a wider audience. These thoughts were the genesis of this book.

In 2017, I began this project by watching two DVDs of lectures he had given for the World War II Lecture Institute. This institute, active from 1997 to 2017 in the Philadelphia area, had its inception at the Abington Free Library in Abington, Pennsylvania and, in 2003, became a partner of the Veterans History Project sponsored by the American Folklife Center of the Library of Congress.

In the first video, recorded on February 16, 1999, my grandfather details his capture and subsequent time in Stalag XI-B. His second lecture, recorded on January 28, 2004, more broadly outlines the timeline from his departure to Europe from New York Harbor to his return to the United States six months later. It also offers an account of his visit to Europe with other veterans for the fiftieth anniversary of D-Day in 1994. I transcribed these lectures, which now form the foundation of this book.

Still, I had more questions. I drove frequently to his

house with my computer to work through them with him. Sometimes I brought printed versions with my questions and comments written in and left them for him to write out answers, fill in holes, and make revisions. When I came back to pick them up, I found each page decorated with lines, arrows, and annotations. He corrected spelling, shifted sentences, and attached pages of reworded passages. As for my questions, more often than not, he simply crossed them out. My favorite comment to make was also his favorite to ignore: "Add more detail!" My main task was to sew together his many comments and disconnected stories into a single, cohesive, and mostly chronological narrative. I reorganized passages and added transitions. However, I remained as eager as ever for more material, so we also continued our interviews. I commented. He responded. I incorporated his responses and added more comments. We carried on for a while—until everything changed.

On July 23, 2018, my grandfather died at age ninety-three. Our work was left unfinished, and I let this project fade into the background as I mourned the loss, focused on my studies at Susquehanna University, and traveled to Freiburg, Germany for a semester abroad, working toward an undergraduate degree in German Studies and Theater Studies. My time in Europe led me to imagine time and again what it might have been like when he had been there—seventy-three years earlier and under thoroughly different circumstances.

In my final year of university studies, under the supervision and guidance of my academic advisor, Dr. Martina Kolb, I completed my capstone project in German Studies. My topic was translation theory with a focus on a lost German Soldier on the Eastern Front in World War II and his letters to his family back in Germany. I selected and translated one of his letters. This German soldier, Adolf Lohmann, reminded me of my grandfather. Both were infantry soldiers in the same war, wrote letters home, and went missing in action. The difference is that my grandfather was rescued from a Nazi prison camp, returned home, and lived a full life. Adolf Lohmann was lost forever. This project gave me a newfound gratitude for my grandfather's life. Lohmann's letters reignited my passion for my grandfather's story and inspired me to continue my preservation of it.

I picked up our work again, determined to finish what we had begun but unsure how to continue without him. No longer able to ask him questions, I was left with the two videos and his pages of comments. I considered his every word change and period placement, working on it occasionally in my free time. Meanwhile, my grandmother sold their house and moved away. It was during this move that I came across two more DVD recordings of him.

The first is an interview he gave for The Art of The American Soldier Exhibit held at the National Constitution Center in Philadelphia from 2010 to 2011. He is featured in his home, seated in his favorite black chair beside an American flag. A woman's voice can be heard off camera, posing questions. Much of what he mentions is also in the original two videos, although with some new details.

The second video was labeled "World War II Lecture Series, Craig Schoeller, Battle of the Bulge, May, 2010" and provides a more extensive recollection of his trip back to Europe in 1994. I later discovered another lecture of his on the World War II Lecture Institute's YouTube channel, recorded on December 19, 2000, and an audio recording of an interview he gave on the Veterans History Project's website dated June 24, 2009.

In his home office, my grandfather kept many documents and relics relating to his time in the war. Not long after his death, I started sorting through them. I came across a collection of letters and Western Union telegrams addressed to his parents, which reveal another dimension of his story. I have interspersed my transcriptions of these chronologically in the main narrative. The transcriptions are literal and deliberately preserve any errors or idiosyncrasies in the originals.

In addition to these, I came across a collection of letters addressed to him by a Dutch woman named Wendy Maesen. In 1998, she wrote him a letter thanking him for helping to free her home city of Venlo before she was born. My grandfather liked to read this letter aloud during some of his lectures. This initial correspondence sparked an exchange between the two that lasted over a decade. In the latter years of their communication, they switched from postal mail to email. Using the email address on her printed messages, I reached out to Wendy in November 2020, explaining who I am, that my grandfather had died, and asking her whether I might use her first letter to him in this book. To my surprise, she not only responded with her permission but suggested that we meet in person the next time I am in Europe. The following year I had the opportunity to do just that.

In September 2021, I moved to Germany as a result of my acceptance into the Fulbright U.S. Student Program administered by the U.S. Department of State. I received the Fulbright English Teaching Assistant Award and spent ten months working at a high school in Kaiserslautern, Germany. During this time, I had the pleasure of visiting Wendy and her family at her home in North Rhine-Westphalia, Germany. Both curious about my grandfather's story, we spent hours searching for the location of his capture outside of Kamp-Lintfort. However, perhaps due to changes in the landscape, we were unable to find an area that matches his description.

Not only does her initial letter to my grandfather display the personal importance of the Allied victory, but their resulting exchange is indicative of the powerful effects of remembrance and its ability to bring people together. This letter can be found in Appendix B, followed by my literal transcription.[1]

Yet still, I uncovered more letters. My grandfather told his story at many different venues during the latter years of his life and was given the opportunity to speak at local high schools through the Veterans in the Classroom Program, created by the World War II Lecture Institute. He received

---

[1] A bibliography has been added following the appendices to indicate sources that were helpful in the presentation of my grandfather's story. In the case of a broken link, all online sources have been archived on https://archive.org/web/.

seventy-nine letters from students over the years, thanking him for sharing his experiences. Although I have not included them in this book, they are meaningful tributes to his story and have informed my preservation of it.

In our time together, I asked my grandfather whether there were any stories about his war experiences he had never told me. He indeed had a few and compiled a list of words and phrases to remind himself of each one during my visits. Unfortunately, he had died before we made it through the list. As a result, some of his memories will remain untold. I list here the ones that did not get told so that they may live on and take shape in our imagination: wild pigs, salute freedom-fighter vets, dug-out, sign up for Korea?

We discussed a title only in passing, and we could never seem to find a suitable one. I had thought to repurpose the title of the blue folder project, but "A Soldier's Story" seemed too generic. After his death, I noticed that one of his DVDs bore the words, "The Ardennes Remembered." I felt this title was right for this book. The Ardennes Counteroffensive, also known as the Battle of the Bulge, was where Hitler made his last offensive push in one of the most significant battles of World War II. For my grandfather, it is the region in which he fought, was wounded, and to which he returned fifty years later. Finally, it is the act of remembering that makes this book possible.

Over the years, my grandfather's memory may well have been altered by time, causing details to be added, lost, or changed. Although rare, I did find a few contradictions in his descriptions. As a result, I had to make editorial decisions, selecting one over the other or editing them together into a general account. However, it has always been of great importance to me to remain as faithful to his words as I possibly could. His recollections are subjective. Therefore, this book does not aim to provide an objective description of history but rather a glimpse into the mind of one who experienced it.

According to his memory, everything that follows is true.

Brian Herrmann

Prologue

December 8, 1941—our lives would change. They filed us into an assembly hall at Olney High School in Philadelphia. All the classes were collected to hear President Franklin Delano Roosevelt deliver a radio address.

> Yesterday, December 7, 1941—a date which will live in infamy—the United States of America was suddenly and deliberately attacked by naval and air forces of the Empire of Japan. The United States was at peace with that nation and, at the solicitation of Japan, was still in conversation with its government and its emperor looking toward the maintenance of peace in the Pacific. Indeed, one hour after Japanese air squadrons had commenced bombing in the American island of Oahu, the Japanese ambassador to the United States and his colleague delivered to our Secretary of State a formal reply to a recent American message. And while this reply stated that it seemed useless to continue the existing diplomatic negotiations, it contained no threat or hint of war or of armed attack. It will be recorded that the distance of Hawaii from Japan makes it obvious that the attack was deliberately

planned many days or even weeks ago. During the intervening time, the Japanese government has deliberately sought to deceive the United States by false statements and expressions of hope for continued peace. The attack yesterday on the Hawaiian Islands has caused severe damage to American naval and military forces. I regret to tell you that very many American lives have been lost. In addition, American ships have been reported torpedoed on the high seas between San Francisco and Honolulu. Yesterday, the Japanese government also launched an attack against Malaya. Last night, Japanese forces attacked Hong Kong. Last night, Japanese forces attacked Guam. Last night, Japanese forces attacked the Philippine Islands. Last night, the Japanese attacked Wake Island. And this morning, the Japanese attacked Midway Island. Japan has, therefore, undertaken a surprise offensive extending throughout the Pacific area. The facts of yesterday and today speak for themselves. The people of the United States have already formed their opinions and well understand the implications to the very life and safety of our nation. As Commander in Chief of the Army and Navy, I have directed that all measures be taken for our defense. But always will our whole nation remember the character of the onslaught against us. No matter how long it may take us to overcome this premeditated invasion, the American people in their righteous might will win through to absolute victory. I believe that I interpret the will of the Congress and of the people when I assert that we will not only defend ourselves to the uttermost but will make it very certain that this form of treachery shall never again endanger us. Hostilities exist. There is no blinking at the fact that our people, our territory, and our interests are in grave danger. With confidence in our armed forces, with the unbounding determination of our people, we will gain the inevitable triumph—so help us God. I ask that the Congress declare that since the unprovoked and dastardly attack by Japan on Sunday, December 7, 1941, a state of war has existed between the United States and the Japanese empire.

An air of fear and stillness connected everyone in the assembly hall. Our futures were in doubt. But the country was together. The Republicans, Democrats, and media were all moving in the same direction. In the hours following the speech, Congress declared war on the Empire of Japan. On December 11, 1941, Germany and Italy declared war on the United States of America.

ONE

I was born on January 15, 1925, in Philadelphia, Pennsylvania. I grew up in Olney in North Philadelphia and am the only child of John and Edna Schoeller. As a boy, my parents took a great interest in my education and welfare. I received a lot of love. They taught me to work hard, save my money, and not to get into debt.

I was also close with my grandparents, who all came from Germany as teenagers. My paternal grandfather moved to the United States when he was fifteen and lived with a distant relative who found him housing and a job as an apprentice clock maker. He learned how to make and repair clocks. With that knowledge, he found jobs at leading firms in Philadelphia like Bailey Banks & Biddle. He went out to homes of people in Chestnut Hill and repaired clocks on sight. He saved his money and when he had enough, he opened his own little shop in downtown Philadelphia, which he later passed on to my father.

My maternal grandfather also came over as a teenager and was good with his hands. He found work with the Frankford Arsenal in the optical department, and he worked on range finders and other pieces of equipment. They were frugal, hardworking, and industrious people.

Back in those days we had the Depression, so we didn't have a lot of money. My dad sold clocks, watches, and jewelry, but people weren't buying those things too much in those times, so he concentrated his business on repair work and that carried him through the Depression. My grandfather had a motto: "Never let a costumer leave the store without a smile on his face." My dad had compassion too. Back in those days people would sell their wedding rings for money and he kept the rings and their addresses. When the economy improved, he let the people know he had their rings. He made a lot of friends that way.

The neighborhoods back then were safe. You didn't have to worry about crime. You didn't have to lock your door. You stayed home and you played games. Families were close together because there weren't many other things to do.

I had at least seven friends within three blocks. We played in the streets. In the summer, we were out playing wireball. We made our own amusement. They were happy days. We didn't have a lot, but it was fun.

As for my education, I attended Morrison Elementary School, Olney Elementary School, and later went on to Olney High School. After graduating from Olney High School in 1942, I entered the Towne Scientific School at the University of Pennsylvania to study mechanical engineering. My aim was to become an officer in the Army Corps of Engineers, so I joined the Reserve Officers' Training Corps. When the United States began drafting for the war, I was deferred because I was still in college. However, after two years, in 1944, my deferment was cancelled, and I was drafted.

By train, I traveled to Camp Blanding, Florida, about fifty miles west of St. Augustine, the oldest city in the U.S. It was hot, humid, and crawling with mosquitos and snakes. I would be there for sixteen weeks, training for the horrors of Europe.

In a way, I was prepared for basic training. I had gone to YMCA camp for about six summers, so I was used to sleeping in a tent and living with the guys. My ROTC training also helped. In fact, sometimes activities in basic training were boring and repetitive because I already knew them.

We slept in tents. There were about twelve of them, six men in each. The interior consisted of simply a cot and a wooden floor beneath it. During the day, we ran obstacle courses where we crawled through dirt as they set off explosions to prepare us for our impending reality. The object was to get through the course without getting dirt in your rifle.

We had to learn about all the weapons: M1 Carbines, machine guns, mortars, etc. Some days we marched out ten miles, set up mortars, fired them all day, and then marched back. It was in the heat of summer. There was always an ambulance following us, picking up the guys who had passed out. We called it the "meat wagon."

The food wasn't too bad. I gained weight. Although, some of the things were a little odd. One cook served spaghetti with his hands. There was also a mess sergeant who filled the sugar bowls with salt. He sold the sugar on the black market until they caught him. But generally, if you had a meal that wasn't too tasty, you went down to the PX (post exchange) at night and loaded up with candy bars.

I made a few friends while I was there. There was a fellow studying engineering at the University of Pennsylvania at the same time I was. Another one was at Drexel. A third fellow was from Virginia. The four of us were pretty close. But another guy, Mark Sherman, and I were always looking for fun. We got together and started rumors to see how they would work their way around camp. We found amusement in that.

Now and then, we had maneuvers at night. One time, our squad was supposed to set up an ambush for the rest of the company moving down the road. We started off through the woods and swamps. It was dark, and the last fellow in line stepped off the path into quicksand. The more he struggled, the deeper he went. Eventually, he was down to his waist. We looked around, found a tree branch, and held it out to him. He grabbed on and we pulled and tugged. We were able to get him out. But we were scared.

Another time, a whole company of us, about two hundred, stood out in a field with our rifles. Our instructions were to hit a target carried by a propeller plane as it flew by. When it passed, we all fired. After they brought the target down, our commanding officers gave us a look of disappointment.

About halfway through basic training, we left camp by foot, heading for the woods. It was about twelve miles until we reached our destination. We constructed tiny two-man bivouac tents in which we would sleep for about two weeks.

One day during this camping trip, the skies turned dark and the wind began blowing furiously. We figured it would be a good idea to hammer our tent pegs deeper into the ground. There was a hurricane coming. Our lieutenant had not had the foresight to hammer down his pegs, so when the wind began blowing, so did his tent. That tent was swept right off the ground and flew into the air, landing a couple of yards away. It was like watching a bird take flight. It was funny. Nobody liked him.

The hurricane lasted a couple of days and then trucks came and took us back. We were just happy we didn't have to walk. Then we found out why. The camp was hit hard. Electric poles were down, trash littered the streets, branches covered the ground, and tents had collapsed. We spent two days cleaning it up.

Every weekend that we behaved they drove us into St. Augustine. We stayed in a little army camp they had for visitors. We were each given a towel and washcloth. We swam in the ocean and went to restaurants for dinner. We stayed there all weekend. The bus line we used was J.O. Miller, and they were all painted blue.

Once we did an exercise where we went through a grass field with targets, shooting at them as they popped up. When I loaded my gun to fire another shot, I was startled by a large object flying past, inches from my head. I realized in moments that it was a bayonet! The fellow behind me had not fastened it to his gun correctly. The bullet had hit the ring of the bayonet and propelled it forward, nearly hitting me. I wasn't even in the war yet.

When training was over, I was told I would be assigned to the Army Specialized Training Corps at a college to do calculations, which, I later discovered, would be used for the Manhattan Project. However, I had the option to join the infantry instead.

I had to make a choice. I could be an engineer and stay home where it was safe, or I could go to war. I thought about how all my friends would be over there fighting. I thought about how when this was all over, I wanted to be able to face other veterans and know that I had not taken the easier road. I wanted to prove that I had the courage, the strength, and the character to fight for my country. After much contemplation, I sent in my decision.

TWO

Wed, Sept. 6. [1944]
Dear Mom + Dad:

I received the card you sent Tues. night this evening. I guess I felt the same as you did and I couldn't say much then either. I meant to tell you how very glad I was you both came down and how wonderful it was to see you. Things worked out beyond our highest expectations and it couldn't have been better. Our prayers were certainly answered.

You needn't worry about me feeling bad. Last night I had a big lump in my throat but it was gone by morning and I started the old routine again. It just requires a lot of will power, determination, and faith in the future.

When I left for the Army I realized what was coming and I was set for it.

I hope your trip home was pleasant. You certainly have a good idea of war-time traveling conditions now. I guess you'll be resting for a week.

Those four days were certainly swell and I, like you, had a wonderful time, the best time of my life. Time certainly went fast. It was another case of long anticipation and the big time coming and going before you know it.

Now I'll start looking forward to my furlough in November. I know everything will work out just as it did last week. The weeks will fly by and it wont be long before I'll be eating some of those wonderful meals of yours, Mom. You wont hear me complaining anymore. That's one good thing the Army teaches you. That's all for tonight.

Until tomorrow
Your loving son,
Craig[2]

---

[2] All transcriptions in this book are literal and deliberately preserve any errors or idiosyncrasies in the originals.

THREE

I was at Fort Meade in Maryland with the infantry fellows, and we took a troop train on the B&O line to Camp Shanks, a deportation port. We came through Philadelphia around 24th and Chestnut to a station there. We rode along the Schuylkill, across 5th Street, one block away from where I lived. I could see my home. I could see my grammar school. I could see Olney High School. I could see my whole life passing by.

At Camp Shanks on Thanksgiving we had a great meal. We entered the mess hall from the front and a long line wound around the side and back of the building. Soldiers exited through the back door after they had finished their dinner.

A fine rain had been falling earlier. The temperature dropped, so the water froze. When the first man came out of the dining hall, he slipped and fell with arms and legs flailing and his empty mess kit flying. This caused great amusement among the troops waiting in line. There was laughter as more and more men exited with acrobatic tumbles. No one thought of giving warning—it was too much fun. This was typical army humor.

We traveled to Hoboken, New Jersey and took a ferry

to New York Harbor. The day after Thanksgiving of the year 1944, I boarded a troopship. Loud music filled the dock as a band played "Over There." I walked up the gang-plank and thought I had about a fifty-fifty chance of sur-vival. I thought to myself: *It might be five years before I return home.* The task ahead of us was a great one. Germany had to be defeated and then Japan. As we set sail, I looked out at the Statue of Liberty, wondering whether I would ever see her again.

FOUR

[Nov. 14, 1944]
Tues. 9:30
Dear Dad:
This is a man to man talk just between you and I. I didn't want to let Mom know so I addressed this letter to you.

I know the real information on this place now and it's just as I thought, although I didn't say anything last week. This is a Replacement Depot and the last place where you go before the port of embarkation. There is still a slight chance that I might go to a camp here in the country but all indications point to the boat ride. We've been issued all new equipment and plenty of winter clothes.

I don't know how long I'll be here. It might be a few days or even weeks. If I'm here this weekend I can get a pass and come home.

Some of the fellows have received their warning orders allready. I'll write to you as long as I can or if possible telephone. When you don't hear anymore from me you'll know I'm on my way.

I don't know what to do about Mom. Maybe it's best you tell her. In any case do what you think best and write and tell me what to do. In the meanwhile I'll continue my joint letters to you and Mom and say everything's fine and I don't know what's going to happen.

Don't worry about me, Pop. I know you're all with me and I've prepared myself for everything. Write as soon as possible and let me know ~~whoat~~ what to do about Mom.

I have the old chin up and I know everything will work out "OK"

I'll write to you tomorrow

Your son,

Craig

F I V E

The *Thomas H. Barry* was the ship that took me across the
Atlantic. Its original name was the *Oriente*, and it was the
sister ship of the *Morro Castle*, which caught fire and was
beached at Asbury Park in 1934. It was a good ship—the
leading flagship of the convoy. Twelve ships, three lines of
four, plus destroyers at each corner started across the stormy
North Atlantic. The destroyers protected us for thousands
of miles from the U-boats.

We passed the Azores, reached the coast of Spain, came
through the Strait of Gibraltar, and anchored in the Mediterranean. All but Morocco's lights were out along the coasts
on account of the war. Morocco wasn't in the war, and I
could see the glow of its shore across the Mediterranean.

We stayed anchored for a few days and then started off
again. I thought perhaps we were going to Italy, but instead
we began veering northeast past the Balearic Islands and
landed at the ancient port of Marseille, France.

We went by truck to the outskirts of the city to an
army camp. We were waiting in a pyramidal tent and were
there no more than an hour when we spotted hands reaching under the flaps of the tent. We soon realized it was a
Frenchman trying to steal our supplies! Groups of our men

raced outside and chased the Frenchman across the field, throwing bayonets at him. I thought: *Here we are protecting your country and you're stealing from us.*

The following day, we moved to a railhead and boarded a train. The train had about twenty boxcars—the same as the ones used in World War I to transport Pershing's American Expeditionary Force. On one of the cars, the following words were stenciled: "HOMMES 40 CHEVAUX 8" (40 MEN 8 HORSES). Well, although we didn't have horses in our boxcar, we had at least forty men and it was crowded. We had to sleep standing up because we couldn't even lie down.

We started northward through the Rhône Valley. I looked out the doors and saw vineyards, terraced landscapes, and many little villages with orange-tiled roofs. We went through Avignon, which was once the home of popes. We passed Lyon and Dijon. The train barreled along at about fifty miles an hour. Sometimes we stopped for a couple of hours and other trains would pass by loaded with tanks, trucks, and supplies for the war. Sometimes we stopped in a little town and the men would go into a bakery and come back with arms full of French bread. Other times I saw men squatting in fields. When the whistle blew, the fellows pulled up their trousers and tried to get to the train in time, but some didn't make it. I imagine Military Police picked them up along the way. Most of the time we just looked at the scenery, kept quiet, and thought about what was to come.

There were two men in our boxcar who did a lot of

talking. They spoke about their fathers and uncles in World War I and bragged about how they were going to "show the Germans." They were excited to get into battle. We told them to shut up.

For three days we rode that train, finally arriving in the town of Toul. From the station, we marched up a big hill to the barracks. It was a couple of hundred years old, probably built by Napoleon and located in a sea of mud—a miserable goo that made it hard to lift your feet. There were about twelve inches of it.

Once in the barracks, it was an adventure to get from the main building to the open-air latrine about a hundred yards away. It was next to the road, and the women from the village went by on their way to the market. As they passed, they got a clear sight of us relieving ourselves. There was very little modesty in France.

We were in Toul for three or four days, sleeping on beds without blankets and pillows. The rooms were small and empty with two people in each one. It was during this time that we received our assignments. I was placed in the 35th Division.

The 35th Division was a part of the Third Army. It landed in Normandy just after D-Day. It fought at Saint-Lô. It fought all the way across France for five months without rest. It was originally a National Guard Division from Nebraska, Missouri, and Kansas. The patch is a Santa Fe cross and a wagon wheel in a field of blue.

I was assigned to the 320th Regiment, Company F, Second Platoon, Third Squad. The veterans of the outfit didn't pay much attention to us. They ignored us because they thought we weren't proven, and they thought that if they got to know us too well, we wouldn't be around long anyway. It was hard being a replacement.

They issued rifles to us. Each man received an M1 Garand rifle. It took us a long time to get the grease off them. Then we went down to the rifle range to zero them in. After we completed that, a green lieutenant lined us up to make sure the chambers were clear of any ammunition. You could tell when someone was a green lieutenant because they didn't have any ribbons yet and their clothes looked new and untattered.

"Inspection arms!" he commanded. At this point, we had to pull our triggers. One fellow pulled the trigger and it discharged. That lieutenant asked contemptuously, "Who fired that shot?" Nobody replied. Nobody confessed. Nobody squealed. The lieutenant said, "Well, you stand there until someone confesses." The rest of us thought we would just wait this guy out. Five minutes passed, then ten. Every once in a while, he ranted and raved. Eventually, it had been forty minutes. The lieutenant finally gave up and marched us back to the barracks. We won.

When we returned to the barracks, another officer told us, "Fellows, you can have a USO show if you can prepare a proper spot." So, we found some lumber in the basement of the barracks and for a day or two we built some benches and a little stage.

When it was completed, we all gathered for the show. The first thing that happened was the brigadier general came out to make an announcement: "Men, the Germans have attacked up north in the Ardennes. A big battle's going on. Soon you'll be there. I know you'll do a good job even though some of you won't make it."

In response, from the back of the room, a fellow from Brooklyn, whose voice was probably trained in the bleachers of Ebbets Field, roared out, "Blow it out your ass, General!" Suddenly, five hundred men jeered, hissed, and booed at that general. He just looked at us and walked off the stage. He couldn't do anything to us. We were going to the front lines the next day.

The show continued with a vocalist, a tap dancer, and an accordion player, but the best part was the general. It was a victory of the enlisted men over a stupid officer.

SIX

The next night, we boarded two-and-a-half-ton trucks and went through the city of Nancy. As we traveled east, I looked out the back and there was a big line half a block long of GIs.

One of the guys yelled, "What's the queue for?"

Another yelled, "It's a cat house!"

We traveled on through Château-Salins. We went through several blasted towns, or deserts rather. In the distance, I could see the flashing and hear the rumbling of artillery coming from eastern France in the Saar Valley.

We pulled into a town called Saint-Jean-Rohrbach near Sarreguemines and bedded down in a one-story farm-house. There was a two-foot hole in the roof. The next morning, we woke up covered in snow.

For a day or so there wasn't too much activity, just an exchange of artillery fire until orders came to move out.

We departed at eleven o'clock at night on December 23. It was about ten degrees. In the trucks, we moved westward, traveling for hours without stopping. I looked back to see a church steeple, a house, or a market. An hour later I saw them again. We were going in circles. I was not sure why. Were we lost? Were the roads crowded? Were we confusing the Germans? Whatever it was, it made for a miserable ride.

We just kept moving. Since they didn't stop, we had to relieve ourselves by using our helmets and passing them out the back. One guy pulled down his trousers, sat on the tailgate, and his flesh froze to the metal. There was not much glory in the infantry, but there sure was a lot of misery.

After eight hours, we reached the city of Metz. Stiff and numb from the ride, we could hardly stand. We got off the trucks and headed into the barracks. The barracks was named Moselle Caserne and had been built by the Germans in 1918. There was no heat or electricity, but we did get a warm meal. Standing in line, I held out my mess kit, and they plopped some mixture of Spam and assorted vegetables on it. I found a comfy spot on the cobblestone street with some men.

It was then when some hungry French kids draped in ragged, filthy clothing approached us. Their hands were cupped and held forward. I went back with a few men to get a second helping and handed it to a kid. They said something to us in French, but of course we couldn't understand. They were grateful and we were glad we could help.

When I had finished eating, I decided to walk across the Moselle River with my friend Phil Robrecht. I met Phil when we were getting our assignments in Toul. A few years older than I, he lived in Delaware on the Chesapeake and was the son of a riverman.

We crossed a small bridge to the other side of town. We were right near a cathedral when we heard gunfire. As we peered around the corner, we saw two GIs about thirty feet apart shooting at each other with .45s just like in the Wild West. They were drunk. A moment later, MPs came, rounded them up, and carted them away.

Phil and I made our way into the old Gothic cathedral. Inside, the air was chilly and the room was damp. That old church had seen a lot of wars. A group of about twelve French women were huddled down in the front of the church praying for the present one to cease.

Walking back from the cathedral, I saw a sign that read "Christmas Eve Service" hanging in the hall of the barracks. We found the lower level decorated with untrimmed fir trees. There was a portable organ, a chaplain, and his assistant, along with about twenty-five men. One of the men passed out song sheets. We sang carols and read scripture.

The chaplain came forward and said, "Fellows, this is a hell of a Christmas, I know. Let me give you a message—a message of hope that Almighty God will see fit to end this conflict and the next Christmas will be a better one for all of us." That made Phil and me feel better.

With renewed spirits, we left the barracks for a breath of fresh air. Outside, we could hear the distant, pulsating drone of a German recon plane followed by anti-aircraft fire. We were back in the war.

SEVEN

Dec. 25, 1944

Dear Mom + Pop:

Merry Christmas! It seems so funny saying those words this year when we're so far apart. Despite the distance, however, I feel that we are together in spirit, not only on this Christmas day but every day. It's so much I could say but I think we understand each other well enough to just let things go unspoken. I'm sorry I couldn't get you any presents this year but I can send you all my love. I guess it takes a Christmas like this to make us realize just what Christmas means and also to appreciate the things we had We can only hope and pray that next Xmas the three of us will be together just like old times.

I imagine by this time you have heard from me. So far I've received letters from you up to Dec. 5. I'm afraid the packages will take a little while to get here.

Please notice the change in address. I've now joined up with a regular outfit. Some of the old fellows who came over with me are still with me and the other fellows seem like a fine bunch. It'll be a lot better now to be with the same bunch all the time and get to make some real friends who I will always be with.

Last night we had card singing and this morning Christmas services. For dinner today we had turkey and all the trimings.

In case you're wondering how I am, don't worry because I'm fine and everything's ok. I know you understand I can't tell you what I'm doing, I can only say I'm certainly seeing a lot of things and I'll have plenty to tell you when I come home. I hope you also understand that some days I'm too busy to write and that the mail is often lost or tied up.

Please say hello and Merry Christmas to everyone for me. That "everyone" takes in a lot of territory, but you know who I mean. I can't think of anything I need except maybe one of those small fountain pen flashlights and any kind of food you think I would like.[3]

I guess that's about all for now. Despite the fact that I'm away from you this year my thoughts have been back there with you and I feel that I'm a mighty lucky fellow because I have the swellest home and the best mom + pop in the world to come back to.

I'll write again as soon as possible

Your loving son,

Craig

---

[3] These words are underlined in black ink with an "X" at the start of the sentence, probably done by one of his parents for reference when preparing a package to send.

EIGHT

The next day was Christmas. It was cold and miserable. We sat around in the stone barracks and spent our time cleaning rifles and patching up holes in our clothing. We had a tree that wasn't decorated, except maybe with a few pieces of tinsel. The only celebration we had was at dinner. The Army did an excellent job of getting turkey dinners to the troops wherever possible. Immediately afterward, we drew ammunition and grenades, cleaned our weapons, and got ready for the next day.

On December 26, we headed north. That day, elements of our division and the Fourth Armored met up with the 101st Airborne in Bastogne. My friend Tony was with the 101st. We didn't know it at the time, but we were only about six miles apart.

As we went up the road toward Luxembourg, we saw single-car engineering outfits and refugees all heading south. We went around Luxembourg City and into the town of Martelang, twelve miles south of Bastogne. Our K-rations (crackers and cheese) and C-rations (meat and beans) were depleted. We bedded down in the hay loft of a barn. I had a hard time falling asleep thinking about what could happen the next day. I had started dozing off until

105 mm batteries set up behind us. They fired over our heads all night.

The next morning, bright and early, we had breakfast: a can of beans and a cup of coffee. The first town we came to was free of Germans. There were women walking up a hill to a church as the bell was tolling. We bypassed that town.

We came to the next town called Bigonville. As we pulled into the town, the Germans were moving out from the other side. We had two tanks with us from the Fourth Armored Division. They were slipping and sliding on the icy roads, but we laid down some boards under the treads and got them moving again. They only made it about half a mile because it was getting too steep.

Our recon outfit went ahead to see if they could locate the Germans. We waited about twenty minutes until they reported we could move forward. The dirt road became narrower, fading into a trail. We stumbled down a steep incline toward the Sûre River and made our way across. By the bank of the river was a Panzer (tank) with its treads knocked off and a damaged turret, probably taken out by one of our aircrafts. It looked like it had been set up to guard the crossing.

We eventually came to the town of Boulaide. The Germans were bunkered on the edge of town, so we tried to bypass them. As our squad made our way past, I heard German machine gun fire in the distance. The sound of each shot blended with the next. "Burp...Burp," it sounded. We called them burp guns. Eventually, it ceased. Our men had taken care of it.

We stopped in a part of town that appeared untouched by the war. When it started getting late, everyone just picked a house to sleep in. I moved into a house behind a church with two other guys, and we found a Luxembourgish woman, about thirty-years old. She came down the stairs as we inspected her house for weapons and German soldiers. She wasn't very friendly, and it was clear we were intruders in her home.

I saw a helmet from the First World War in the closet. I picked it up to examine it and showed it to her. She said, "1914, schlechtes Jahr" (bad year). She let us sleep on the floor that night.

NINE

The next day, on December 28, we were in battalion reserve. The 101st Airborne was encircled up by Bastogne. Our goal was to relieve them. The following day, on the 29th, we moved out of Boulaide and into the attack.

A couple of hundred yards outside of Boulaide, I saw a German officer sitting against a tree. I thought: *Why isn't this officer being guarded?* When I moved closer, I could see why. His face was covered with frost and his blue eyes were wide open, staring eastward to Germany—the home he would never see again. The sight of that officer made us all aware of our own mortality as we went down that road not knowing what was going to happen. In the infantry, nobody told you what your objective was; you just moved ahead and reacted.

Farther down the road, we came to a farmhouse and rested. We waited there awhile until the brass badges decided what we were going to do. We didn't have tanks because they weren't able to get across the river, and our artillery was occupied in other sectors. It was strictly an infantry operation.

Later, we found out that the First SS Panzer Division was in front of us as well as the 167th Volksgrenadier

Division—two good German outfits. On our right flank was the 26th Division and on our left flank was the Fourth Armored. The whole Third Army was moving ahead, putting pressure on the southern flank of the Bulge.

We left the farmhouse and, after a mile or so, came to a crossroads. There were about ten foxholes, each one a grave holding a casualty. These were fellows from G Company that had set up a roadblock and had been killed by artillery fire. We just walked gingerly around them without staring.

There appeared to be a lot of air activity. I saw our Piper Cubs doing recon, P-47s and Messerschmitts dogfighting in the sky, and B-17 bombers on their way to hit the German supply lines. Then we received orders to extend to our left flank and move up about a hundred yards. That's when all hell broke loose.

TEN

We heard the rumble just before the 88 mm shells rained down upon us. The 88 was the Germans' best field piece. It had a high muzzle velocity. You could hear it screaming just before it hit you. There was hardly any time to react. In moments, there were several casualties.

We tried moving toward the woods to get into a better position, away from the 88s. As we did that, there was an explosion of machine gun and rifle fire. We dived for cover behind nearby trees. Our khaki and olive drab made for easier targets than the white tunics and garments the Germans were wearing. After much exchange of fire, however, they seemed to be retreating. We had them outnumbered and on the run.

Somebody called out, "Watch out for snipers!" As the Germans were pulling back, snipers were covering their retreat. We trudged through a foot of snow as we ran toward them. When a gap formed between us and them, German mortars rained down on top of us. I hit the ground.

I continued stumbling through the ice and snow, dodging the explosions. As we chased the Germans up the hill, I passed bodies on the ground, among them, the two boisterous fellows from the train. One was holding the bloody stump of his arm; the other was face down in a blanket of snow. So, they showed them.

The shells continued to drop from the sky, some hitting the earth and others the trees. I fell flat on my face. There was an indentation in the ground, and I rolled over into it, pressing down as tightly as I could. The earth shook, and I could smell the cordite.

Finally, it stopped. In the diminished noise, I heard my friend Phil crying out in pain. I spotted him about twenty feet away and raced over. He was hit in the chest and in both legs. I called out for a medic and in moments one was there. He gave Phil a shot of morphine, and we cut open his clothes and put sulfa powder on his wounds. Litter-bearers carried him away. The next time I saw him, we would be home.

It was then I noticed a severe pain in my right thigh. I had been hit too.

The sound of machine gun fire cracked through the air again. I fell to the ground and crawled through the snow, down a little draw. Then there was silence. Someone probably threw a grenade at him.

What was left of our platoon was following the Germans to find out where they were going. I went with them. After about half a mile, we stopped for a minute. I used this opportunity to call over the medic.

"Better take a look at my leg," I said. I was wearing two pairs of GI trousers and long johns. I peeled them off, and sure enough, there were two bloody holes.

He looked and said, "Oh yeah, you got hit. Whenever

you get a chance, go back to the aid station." We went another half mile when orders came over the radio to return to the main line of resistance.

It was getting dark and I didn't know where the aid station was. I was afraid to wander because of German patrol and trigger-happy GIs, so I decided to wait until morning.

ELEVEN

Since Phil was wounded and gone, my new foxhole buddy was a Native-American fellow, perhaps an Apache or a Ute from the southwestern states. But he was no Geronimo. Together, we had to start digging a foxhole to protect us from the artillery.

Despite my lethargy, I said, "Okay, let's start digging." He sat down under a tree and grunted. Frustrated, I urged, "Come on, chief! This is going to save our butts. Let's start digging!" He didn't say a word. He had just given up. He didn't want any more of the white man's war, I guess. Alone, I grabbed a shovel, found a spot with a good field of fire, and started digging.

There was a foot of snow, and beneath it, the ground was frozen and packed with rocks and tree roots. It was like digging in concrete. We had a little entrenching tool. It was like a shovel, but you could move the blade ninety degrees to make it into a pick. Hour after hour, I picked away at the dirt in subfreezing temperature. It was miserable, but I knew I had to do it because it might save my life. I also knew that if I fell asleep, I would freeze to death.

At ten o'clock at night, the roaring motors of two tank destroyers captured my attention. They came to the top of the hill and started firing in the direction of the German lines. When the Germans returned fire, instead of hitting the TDs, the counterfire landed short on top of us. That spurred me on to dig a little faster. But the TDs eventually departed and the counterfire ceased.

At midnight, coffee made its way around. It wasn't Jamaican or Colombian; it was black and the only thing I had in my stomach since the beans and coffee that morning. It was delicious.

I went back at it all night long, just scraping and digging. By dawn, I was down about three and a half feet. It took about twelve hours—just in time for the mortars to come in.

The Germans were trying to saturate the whole area. They started dropping shells in a grid pattern—firing a shell, moving over twenty-five feet, firing, then another twenty-five feet. They moved across the row and went again the other way. You could tell when a shell was coming into your area, and it was a relief as it passed down the line. They made about three or four cycles like that and then stopped.

I figured now was a good time to try to get to the aid station. My leg was stiff and in pain. I picked up my rifle, dragged my leg out of the foxhole, and started crawling through the snow. The tips of my fingers were poking through my flimsy knit gloves. I dug them into the snow to pull myself forward. After about two hundred yards, I started to wonder if I was going to make it.

Then, by dumb luck, the captain came along in his

jeep! He and his driver lifted me up and put me in the back of the vehicle. We rode for about a mile, eventually reaching a town called Baschleiden. The aid station was in a two-story house. They gave me a shot for tetanus. There were two other fellows there waiting for the ambulance when we heard a shell come in. This time it was bigger than 88s, probably 240s. The Germans had a railroad gun near Bastogne, and it was firing in our direction.

The shell hit a house and the whole thing came tumbling down. Then, farther down the street, another shell came in. The Germans had discovered there was an aid station in town.

When the ambulance arrived, they loaded it with one fellow on a stretcher, and the rest of us piled in. The driver zigzagged through the rubble and shell fire. The whole town was collapsing. We raced back through Boulaide and crossed the Sûre River. Luckily, the engineers had put up a Bailey bridge, so we could cross.

We stopped at another aid station and picked up two officers who had been hit by flying glass. Their heads were completely bandaged. We helped them into the ambulance and headed toward the field hospital located in Longwy, France.

At the hospital, they took an X-ray of my leg. My right thigh had two major pieces of shrapnel about the size of a thumbnail right next to the bone. By luck, no major blood vessels were hit. I waited an hour until I was taken into the operating room. There were six tables with doctors and nurses at each one. It was like the show *M*A*S*H*. Blood stained the floor and walls. The wounded came in as the bandaged came out. It was like an assembly line. The staff was certainly very serious, and they were doing a wonderful job.

They gave me a shot of sodium pentothal to numb my pain and knock me out. I remember counting to about seven before my mind faded. I woke up the next morning with a bandage on my leg, lying on a bed out in the hall. Later, they took me down to a railroad siding because there was no room in the hospital. I stayed in a tent that night.

The next morning, the hospital train came in to take me to a general hospital. It was painted khaki with big red crosses on the top and sides of the cars. We rode about sixty-five miles from Longwy, France to Commercy, France.

T W E L V E

Winter, 1945. A Western Union boy on a bike delivered a telegram to my father's house:

1945 JAN 16 PM 12 23
REGRET TO INFORM YOU YOUR SON PRI-
VATE CRAIG A SCHOELLER WAS SLIGHTLY
WOUNDED IN ACTION THIRTY DECEMBER
IN LUXEMBOURG YOU WILL BE ADVISED AS
REPORTS OF CONDITION ARE RECEIVED
DUNLOP ACTING THE ADJUTANT GENERAL.

THIRTEEN

The general hospital was in an old French school. It was warm, clean, and the food was adequate. I was just happy to be alive and out of the snow. I recall there were sixteen fellows in our ward. All had grey toes from frostbite, including me. It didn't help that our toes stuck out from the sheets on our beds. We had to massage them daily to get the circulation back. Many men lost their toes. I was lucky.

During the day, we read detective novels, Westerns, and *Stars & Stripes*, the Army newspaper. We also enjoyed listening to the BBC on the radio. They played good music—Harry James, the Dorseys, Glenn Miller, Benny Goodman, Artie Shaw, and all the other famous bandleaders. Dinah Shore sang "I'll Walk Alone" and Vera Lynn sang "The White Cliffs of Dover."

Sometimes we turned on the German radio. They played "Lili Marlene" and American music but always interspersed with propaganda. They said, "You Americans are being slaughtered in Belgium. 4Fs are seducing your wives and sweethearts at home." But that didn't have any effect on us. Joseph Goebbels didn't understand the American soldier. We used their propaganda as jokes. At night, however, sometimes fellows had nightmares and would

— 36 —

talk and scream in their sleep.

There were a couple of German orderlies who worked in the hospital. These were older men in their fifties. One of the men accidently knocked a glass over and broke it. He started shaking and was upset. I had German in high school and I didn't have a big vocabulary, but I was able to tell him, "Don't be afraid. Everything will be alright." Then we talked for a little bit, and he told me that he had a brother who was killed in the First World War and two sons still serving in the German Army.

I was born on January 15, 1925. I reached my twentieth birthday in that hospital. There were no cards, no cakes, and no presents. Because of moving around, I didn't receive any mail for two months after I had left the States. But what was most disheartening was the uncertainty of a twenty-first. I just hoped for a happier birthday in the future. It was a sad time.[4]

Near the end of the month, they took out my stitches, and orders came down from Third Army headquarters: "All walking wounded back to the front." I left with a bandage and a limp.

---

[4] During every celebration of my grandfather's birthday that I can remember, he recalled this day in a speech to our family and gave thanks.

FOURTEEN

Jan. 15, 1945
Dear Mom + Pop:
Well today marks twenty years since your little bundle of joy arrived. Like Christmas and other days we'll have to let the celebration go until later when we really have something to celebrate about.

A lot has happened in those twenty years. I've grown from a tiny, little runt to a great, big, clumsy lug and I guess I've given you a number of headaches along the way, but they've been years in which you've given me everything that a mother and father could give their son. I really appreciate the things you've done for me and all the sacrifices you've made and I hope you're as proud of me as I am of you.

I'm still taking things easy here in the hospital. My wound is coming along fine and I'll say again that it is not serious and nothing at all to worry about.

I'll write again soon.
Your loving son,
Craig

FIFTEEN

Jan. 24, 1945

Dear Mom + Dad:

Still about the same news. My wound in the leg is coming along fine and I feel swell. Yesterday I got my first haircut since I left the States. It was getting so long that I was starting to look for a fiddle. It certainly feels a lot better now.

Here's something I'd like for you to do for me. Take a five spot out of the money I sent home and either on a weeknight or Sunday take in a dinner at Beck's and a movie afterwards. Don't forget and take the expenses from my money and have a good time on me.

I'll write again soon.

Your loving son,

Craig

SIXTEEN

Jan. 30, 1945

Dear Dad:

Thought I'd write this letter especially to you. One of these days I'll be leaving the hospital and going back to duty. You know what that means. In any case I'll be in there doing my best and looking out for myself. You can tell where I'm at by reading about the Third Army and the Thirty fifth Division.

I hope Mom is taking things okay and I know you're cheering her up. Tell her anything to ease her mind and I'll be writing as often as possible.

Don't worry, God will watch over me.

Your pal and son,

Craig

SEVENTEEN

From the general hospital in Commercy, we traveled by truck to Vaucouleurs, where our replacement depot was on the main street. Joan of Arc had once been there. There were other troops coming back from the hospital to join up with forces.

Across the street, I spotted a public shower. I hadn't had a shower in two months, so I figured it would be a nice treat. My last one was a cold saltwater shower on the ship.

I paid ten francs to the madam, went across the room, took off my clothes, and entered a stall. She turned on the water and I soaped up. Well, for ten francs I didn't get much water, and I was surprised when it suddenly shut off. So, I had to leave the stall, shuffle across the room, get ten francs, walk over to the madam, and go back into the stall. Again, not much modesty in France. I didn't have another shower for three months. It was a dirty war.

From Vaucouleurs we rode boxcars through Verdun, where there were about one million casualties in World War I. Later, we arrived at another replacement depot near Metz and rested for the night in a large building. The next morning, a sergeant came in and grabbed a few of us for a detail.

The job was to clean out a stable of straw and manure to make living quarters for troops coming in. With a new buddy from the group, I picked up my shovel and started hauling the manure. A few minutes into this degrading task, I exclaimed, "This is beyond our dignity!" We decided that two combat infantrymen shouldn't be shoveling manure. Dropping our shovels, we shimmied up the wall, went through a little window at the top, and jumped down the other side. We didn't want to take the chance of an officer seeing us go through the door.

It was a large compound. After walking about a hundred yards, we stumbled upon a collection of German equipment, field guns, and other items. Suddenly, we heard a hissing sound. Sharing a glance, we hit the ground, bracing ourselves for a booby trap. But only silence followed. Rising cautiously, we discovered that the source was nothing more than a leaking air cylinder. For a moment, we thought we were being punished for shortening our job of shoveling manure.

As we continued, we heard some commotion in a nearby building. We found a USO group having a quiz contest. The topics were American history and geography—two subjects that were right up my alley. My knowledge served me well because I ended up winning a round. My prize was a big box of candy bars: Hershey, Mr. Good, and Baby Ruths. I brought it back to the barracks. I was a big hero.

EIGHTEEN

Feb. 23, 1945

Dear Mom:

Happy Birthday! I'm sorry I can't be home with you to celebrate this year but I'm with you in thought anyway. I know how you must feel with me being away and I want you to know that I'm allways thinking of you and Dad. You're the swellest Mom in the world and I really appreciate all the things you've done and are doing for me. I think we understand each other well enough, so I needn't say more.

Happy Birthday again, Mom, and let's pray that next year I can say those words in person.

All my love,

Craig

NINETEEN

The next day, we moved again—this time by truck. We made our way north because the 35th Division had been transferred from the Third Army to the Ninth Army for reinforcement.

We went right through the area of the Bulge. We passed through Thionville, Arlon, Harlange, Bastogne, and Houffalize. It was the same route I had taken just after Christmas. For seventy miles there were shot-up tanks, trucks, jeeps, halftracks, downed wires, fallen trees, and destroyed equipment. There was rubble in the place of churches and houses, utter desolation. Mile after mile. It was unbelievable.

We went through Liège and headed north to a little town called Sint-Truiden. There, we found a theater and saw a movie called *Gaslight* with Charles Boyer and Ingrid Bergman.

The following day, we headed to Maastricht and stopped there for the night along the Maas River. The Meuse River starts in France and ends as the Maas River in Holland. The British were with us in Maastricht. We were supposed to sweep our side of the river as the British swept the other side, trying to push the Germans back.

We had to wait for another group to come up. I remember resting on the steps of a house when a Dutch boy, about sixteen years old, sat next to me.

"I'd like to give you a souvenir to send to your mother," he told me, retrieving a small metal object from his pocket. He placed it in my hand. Observing it more closely, I saw that it was Queen Wilhelmina on a Dutch coin, except he had cut out a silhouette between the head of the queen and the rim of the coin. On the back, he had soldered a pin. It was the nicest little thing. I thanked him for it.

As we continued to talk, I started to hear the intermittent hum of a V-1 (buzz bomb) overhead. The bomb was headed toward us, flames shooting out the back. Chugging along, it passed over our heads. We watched with trepidation. After flying another quarter of a mile, its engine cut out and it came crashing down in a tremendous explosion. We were so happy it missed us.

I thought: *Well, I'm glad they don't have those up at the front.* Apparently, it was headed for Antwerp but ran out of fuel and fell short.

From Maastricht, we went again by truck, this time finally joining the division along the Roer River. The Germans had blown up some dams and flooded the valley, and the American troops were waiting for the water level to go down before making an assault.

I saluted the captain. He remembered me and said, "Glad to have you back with us." He was a good guy. Company F, 320th had eleven captains from July of 1944 until May of 1945. He lasted longer than any of them—five months.

It often occurred that when you left the hospital you didn't return to your original unit, but that wasn't the case for me. There were about 180 men that had left Metz the day after Christmas. I only recognized about forty faces now. The ranks were filled with replacements and men who had returned from being wounded in northern France. From the Third Squad, everyone was gone: the squad leader, the assistant squad leader, the BAR (Browning Automatic Rifle) man, the medic, my friend Phil, the Native-American, and two others. I was the only survivor. The rest were either killed, wounded, or frostbitten.

In that short time, I received my baptism of fire. Like Stephen Crane's *Union Soldier*, it was a red badge of courage. I became a veteran, made new friends, and started off on new adventures.

I remember getting into a jeep with a cook. We were taking food down to a town along the Roer. When we arrived, the cook took the food out, dropped it, jumped back in the jeep, and zoomed out. I wondered why he had left so fast. But a minute later, a shell came in and landed right where the jeep had been.

One adventure happened while I was on duty at an outpost along the Roer with two other guys. We were watching the Germans across the river and taking turns getting chow. The kitchen was about seven hundred yards up the road of a bombed town. Eventually, my turn came.

The Germans had good observation and communication. They also had so much artillery that they would fire at one man. So, as I walked through the town, I had made it about halfway before I heard an 88 mm shell coming. I scanned the area for cover. I noticed a house on the other side of the street with a destroyed side wall. A cast-iron bathtub stood in the exposed room. I bounded across the street and dived into the tub as the shell came in. It landed in the middle of the street about twenty-five feet away. I heard the clank of shrapnel striking the metal side. I was saved by a bathtub. Ever since, I have always had a soft spot in my heart for them. When it was over, I got out and continued to the chow line.

Another adventure started in a town we were sweeping for Germans. A few guys went into a barn and came out with a chicken. It was squawking and the guy holding it swung it around and broke its neck. We were happy to have something to eat.

Then a German man about seventy years old in a house about seventy yards away stuck his head out of an upper-story window and yelled, "Verdammte Amerikaner!" (Damn Americans!). I aimed my gun at him and clicked the bolt of my rifle. He pulled his head back inside. I wasn't going to shoot. I just wanted him to stop cussing at us.

As we moved from town to town, stopping to search for Germans, we would try to cook the chicken a little each time. We started small fires, taking wood from the rubble of houses or broken fences. This carried on for a few days. Eventually, we stopped at a town that had some sort of rabbit farm. There were hundreds of rabbits enclosed by a little fence. About fifty guys, hooting and hollering, jumped the fence and went wild with these rabbits, shooting and throwing bayonets at them. They had been eating crackers and canned meat for months.

Some other guys and I weren't interested in eating rabbits. We were happy with our chicken. We made another fire and finally finished cooking it. When we bit into it, it was tough and tasteless rubber. I wasn't interested after a few bites.

TWENTY

As the war progressed, we crossed the Roer River, drove farther north into Holland, and broke through the Siegfried Line. We liberated the city of Venlo. As we entered the town on March 2, we were greeted by a jubilant populace. The people emerged from their homes and hiding places. Many came running out waving little orange flags. There were cheers and there were tears. We were gratified. They had been oppressed by the Germans for five years.

Our time for celebration was short-lived. That night, we continued to attack, and I recall the countryside being illuminated by scores of burning haystacks as we moved toward Straelen.

From there, we liberated a few more towns, driving eastward into Germany. We captured the towns of Sevelen and Kamp-Lintfort. I remember a rail siding in Sevelen with a boxcar full of Cognac. Many men took advantage of this good fortune. Although, we would have been in bad shape if the Germans had counterattacked. However, it was in Kamp-Lintfort where we encountered considerable resistance.

As we were moving down the road, we got fired at by our own artillery until they called it off. We finally got to the center of town and the Germans were releasing a terrific barrage of shells. It was really coming in. Then we heard a scream from the street. We looked out and saw it was a German in pain. Our medic went out and pulled the German in and gave him a shot of morphine.

The artillery fire let up a little and we started moving down the street. When more shells came in, we went behind a big coal pile for cover. It was a mining area.

We went house by house looking for Germans. In one house I entered, there was a center hall with doors on both sides. Hearing somebody behind one of the doors, I readied my rifle to fire and waited. The door slowly opened, and an old woman appeared. With relief, I lowered my weapon. I came within seconds of doing something that I would have regretted all my life.

Then we got down farther on the edge of town. A lieutenant told me and a fellow by the name of McGill to round up all the civilians in the area and put them in a big house. Along the street, McGill and I stopped to look at a little German sports car. A bullet came right between us and through the windshield. We moved out of there fast.

We rounded up the civilians and put them in a house. The woman who owned the house was upset, and she opened the windows so the concussions wouldn't break the glass. There were women and some children frying potatoes and they gave us some. They were just glad that we were kind to them.

I started wondering what the other fellows were doing. When they came back, I saw my friend Top Edwards. He had a funny look on his face. I asked him, "What happened?" I noticed everybody was hanging their heads. Our captain, James M. Watkins, and my good friend Brock had been killed by sniper fire. I didn't sleep that night.

TWENTY-ONE

The following day, on March 6, we pushed toward the Rhine River about fifteen miles away. There were twelve Sherman tanks with about ten men on the back of each. We rode in a column and I was on the second tank.

We proceeded into the countryside looking for Germans. Our men shot up haystacks and isolated farmhouses. We were probing, looking for the Germans.

Eventually, we came to a little town. We jumped off the tanks, and I ran into a house and discovered warm food on the table and the back door open, so we knew the Germans had just left.

As we continued advancing, about forty Germans emerged from trenches and foxholes and raised their arms in surrender. We just waved them back to the rear of the column. Farther along, another group of about ten Germans rose out of trenches and started to run. Our tanks just mowed them down with machine guns. That wasn't necessary. But running was such a foolish thing to do. You can't outrun a bullet.

We knew we were coming to the main line of resistance. When we moved to the edge of a little hamlet, we saw a village about a thousand yards away. In front of it was a railroad crossing and no one in sight. It was peaceful. Calm.

We hesitated for a while. Because Captain Watkins had been killed the day before, the tank commander and executive officer were running the show. They did not have as much experience as our captain. They apparently were not sure what to do because we waited about five minutes until the order finally came over for the tanks: "Advance slowly." If our captain had not been killed, he would have called in air and artillery support.

Our column moved ahead. We were apprehensive. I thought it was a trap. We moved cautiously, one after another. Mine fields were on either side, so our tanks couldn't maneuver. They had to stay on the road.

The first tank had just come up on the railroad crossing when the Germans fired. An 88 went into the front of the first tank and right out the back; then came another, hitting the third tank in the turret.

In the chaos, we tumbled off the tanks and ran into a trench by the side of the road. The fellows from the first tank and some of the guys from mine ran forward through a hedgerow and into a house on the other side of the railroad tracks. The rest of the tanks just turned around and scooted back up the hill.

The Germans bombarded us with 88s and mortars. We were hunkered down in the trench as rocks and mud fell on top of us. It continued for a while and then stopped. Absolute silence.

So, there we were. Six of us huddled in: Pop Keller, Kreve, Lewandowski, Slattery, Edwards, and me. All were

PFCs. It was a "V" shaped trench and I was at the apex.

I peeked my head up to see the first tank destroyed, but no Germans. They didn't know we were there. Looking behind me, I saw the third tank in line and no cover for about a thousand yards up the hill.

A half hour had passed when the sound of distant small arms fire and grenades grabbed my attention. We all knew it was coming from the house where our men had taken cover. Our fellows were in there fighting the Germans. The skirmish lasted about ten minutes. Then it was quiet. We knew they were either captured or killed.

Another hour had gone by when suddenly a fellow came out of the hedgerow at the side of the road—one of our men. His nickname was "the Greek." He came running past, but upon noticing us, paused at the trench. Emphatically, we waved him on. The last thing we wanted was to draw attention. I guess he ran up that hill like his ancient forefathers who had run in marathons because, somehow, he made it without being seen. It was miraculous.

That gave us some hope. We now knew our troops up the hill had knowledge of where we were. *What do we do?* I thought. *The Germans don't know we're here. The best option is to wait until dark and crawl back.*

An hour went by. Then another. As darkness fell, we figured if we could hang in there for a few more hours, we could escape. Then a couple of strange things happened.

Two Germans emerged from the town wearing white tunics with big red crosses on the front and back. They approached the first demolished tank. After circling it, they looked inside and found a wounded man. They pulled him out of the hatch and placed him on a stretcher.

In the trench, we had a fellow named Slattery—a lanky guy with big feet and a small brain. Slattery had a sudden, untimely attack of diarrhea. Slipping down his pants, he squatted. The rest of us sat still. As Slattery stood to raise his pants, his helmet poked up from the trench. I was watching from the other side of the "V." One of the Germans caught a glimpse of the motion and they both scurried back into town. Terror, shock, and panic overcame me. We had been discovered.

Two minutes had passed, and about twenty Germans came down with automatic weapons, yelling at us in German, "You in the hole, surrender!"

I said to the fellows, "We are in trouble. What do you want to do?" Nobody said a word. The decision was mine. *What do I do?* I had to make a decision. If I shot a couple of them, we'd all be killed. Then I remembered stories like Malmedy and the American soldiers who had all been killed there after being taken prisoner. We couldn't surrender either. I didn't want to be captured. They kept coming closer.

Then I remembered the Greek had run back. Our troops knew we were there. *Maybe I can get help from the fellows behind.* I decided to act.

I aimed my rifle above and a few feet to the right of the German leader, firing two quick shots. All the Germans dropped to the ground and returned fire. I ducked, moved over a couple of feet, and put my head up again. At the same time, I heard a thunder of shells from behind.

A barrage of smoke shells landed about seventy yards to our left and little ahead of us. They would have helped us had they been on target, but they didn't have time to zero them in. We would have been able to run out, and they could have dropped HEs (high explosives) on top of the Germans.

In the chaos, I noticed a German with a potato masher pulling his arm back. I yelled, "Grenade!" We all ducked. I was waiting for it to come in so I could toss it out. It landed about six feet from my head on the outside of the trench and stuck in the mud. It didn't go off. It was a dud.

We had to decide our next move quickly, and we realized our only chance of survival was to surrender. I took my pen knife, hid it in my boot, and we all stood up with our hands raised before they could throw another. The German that threw the grenade came over, picked it up, and tossed it away in disgust.

Hastily, they took us past the tank and up to the courtyard of a house. There, we met two of our fellows that had been in the house skirmish. One had a bullet wound in the shoulder, and the other had been shot in the leg. The rest of them weren't there.

The Germans lined us up against a wall and stood there with Schmeissers. We didn't know what was going to happen. We were scared to death. Fortunately, they just took our weapons, searched us, and marched us through the town.

I saw they had anti-tank guns, machine gun nests, and

bazookas. The town was well fortified. If the Germans had not been impatient and had let us advance, there would have been a tremendous firefight in that town.

We walked up a small hill to the last house. The other fellows from the house battle were there. None had been killed. It was sort of a mixed group. There were Panzer troops without tanks and paratroopers. All young guys. One of the Germans looked at our patch. He pointed at it and said, "Panzer? Panzer?"

I said, "Kein Panzer. Fünfunddreißig Infanteriedivision" (Not Panzer. Thirty-fifth Infantry Division). They were sort of curious and not too unfriendly. We stayed in the house for about five minutes before the Germans took us out. They piled us in one of those German half-tracks, and we started down the road toward the Rhine.

By that time, our artillery had moved up close enough and spotted the German half-track. We were just outside of the town when one of our 105 mm shells hit in front of the half-track, followed by another behind us. We were bracketed in. The German driver swerved off the road and across a field. The battery fired about five more shells at us. It was bad enough being shot at by the Germans, but when you were shot at by your own men, it wasn't too good. We escaped that and survived.

We came to a little town along the Rhine and they took us into a house. They filed us into the kitchen and one by one brought us into the living room. I was in the middle of the group. As I entered, I saw there was a German lieutenant waiting for me. He must have been about thirty-five years of age. I approached his desk and, saluting him, stated my name, rank, and serial number. I wanted to show him I was a good soldier.

He started asking me questions: "What unit are you with? How long have you been on the front? What was the situation in which you were captured?"

After each question, I told him, "I can't tell you." I figured I didn't have any knowledge he'd want to have anyway. So, I played it by the book. Each time he just nodded. When he was through, he gave me all the answers himself. Either his intelligence was good or somebody else had said something.

He took me over to the door. Placing his hand on my shoulder, he stated proudly, "For you the war is over, soon it will be over for all of us." But my war was far from over. I had a long way to go.

T W E N T Y ˜ T W O

1945 APR 2 PM 7 36

THE SECRETARY OF WAR DESIRES ME TO
EXPRESS HIS DEEP REGRET THAT YOUR
SON PFC SCHOELLER CRAIG A HAS BEEN
MISSING IN ACTION IN GERMANY SINCE SIX
MAR 45 IF FURTHER DETAILS OR OTHER IN-
FORMATION ARE RECEIVED YOU WILL BE
PROMPTLY NOTIFIED

J A ULIO THE ADJUTANT GENERAL.

TWENTY-THREE

When they were finished interrogating us, they marched us down toward the Rhine River. Along the way, we passed a house with a group of Germans inside, drinking, singing, and having a ball—oblivious to the war.

Eventually, we made it to the bank of the Rhine. That part of the river was narrow, but the current was extremely swift. The Germans were preparing to take us across in a motorboat. It was small with about ten horsepower and could only hold half a dozen people. They took us over in shifts.

Abruptly, a British Mosquito Bomber, one of the fastest bombing planes in Europe, shot overhead trying to hit the railroad bridge up north in Wesel. It was bombing the riverbanks along the way. We dodged the bombs for a while.

They sent another group of us across the river. Suddenly, our 155 mm batteries started firing at both sides of the river. Again, we were dodging our own shells. About thirty feet from us, a shell hit in the water. I went down in the mud with a German guard lying next to me. No one was hit. Finally, we got across the river. On the other side, the Germans were dug in, and we continued to dodge shell fire.

We arrived at another small town. When more shells came in, we fell on the cobblestones. One of the shells hit an ammunition dump and it blew up. We just kept dodging shells as we headed deeper into German territory.

We finally stopped and they put us in a barn. We were exhausted. Just as I was about to fall asleep, one of our planes, a P-47, came over and bombed a railroad bridge nearby, blowing the roof off our barn. The horses and cattle got all excited and started to trample some of the fellows. That was another adventure, but we finally got to sleep.

The next day, we joined the German refugees who were leaving the Rhineland and moving inland. They had packs on their backs and were pulling carts and baby coaches and bicycles, scrambling to get away from the war.

We had about twenty-five miles until the train station. As we went along, a girl on a bike, appearing to be in her early twenties, was traveling along the road. Coming from the opposite direction was an SS dispatch rider on a motorcycle in a black leather coat with a black helmet. Tearing up the road and around a bend, he clipped the girl on the bike, sending them both sprawling. He picked up his motorcycle, jumped on, and drove away. He never turned around to see what happened to the girl. We all ran over to help her. Her bike was wrecked. She was bruised and cut but not too badly injured.

Farther down the road, there was a German field kitchen, and the German cooks had just slaughtered a cow, so when they saw us coming, they figured they could get some free labor. They told the German guards to bring us over and handed us ropes that were tied around a big cow. We all threw the ropes over and pulled, raising the cow. For our efforts, we were given a drink of water.

As we trekked on, we didn't walk with our heads down like prisoners. We just strolled along like tourists looking around.

Finally, we arrived at the town of Dorsten. It was a railroad center where we were supposed to catch a train. We passed a compound with slave laborers wearing striped suits. They were waving and yelling at us in some strange language. It sounded like it was from the Balkans. We just waved backed to them.

Then they put us in a waiting room for a while. After some time, a German colonel entered—the Oberst. He was one of those guys you see in Hollywood movies—short hair, scowl, a real Prussian type. He grabbed the roster from our guards, looked at it, and ordered, "Meyer. Schoeller. Wo sind Sie?" So, we went up.

The colonel looked at us and asked, "Warum kämpfen Sie nicht für das Vaterland?" (Why aren't you fighting for the homeland?). We both had German names.

In my high school German, which wasn't that great, I responded, "My grandparents came from Germany to America. My parents were born in America. I was born in America, and I *am* fighting for my homeland."

He just looked at me with disgust and walked away.

TWENTY-FOUR

We boarded the train. It had a car with an anti-aircraft gun and some machine guns on it. During our trip, an Allied plane came over and fired at us. The Germans fired back and we escaped the attack.

The next day, we reached the city of Münster and traveled on to Osnabrück, an ancient city. A Roman legion was wiped out in that area way back in history.

The station was at the intersection of two railroad lines. As soon as we arrived, the air raid sirens sounded. We rushed into the basement of the railroad station as B-17s flew in overhead. We could hear the whistling of the bombs. The earth shook as they released bomb after bomb on the city. The masonry started falling on top of us. Then it ceased.

When we came up to street level, the town was burning. There were bodies everywhere.

TWENTY-FIVE

Since the railroad was knocked out, we had to travel about fifteen miles to the next town by foot. We were back on the road.

As we walked, people spat at us. About a dozen boys on stilts jumped off their stilts and started throwing rocks at us until the guards made them stop.

We finally got to the next railroad station, hopped on the train, and went to Bremen—a major German city.

In Bremen, we waited for the next train. We were accompanied by three German guards: two young boys and an old German sergeant who had been on the Eastern Front. The sergeant had his bike with him because he was going home on leave. He gave me his bike and told me to take it to the baggage car and check it.

As I walked to check the bike, I saw Wehrmacht troops, SS troops, and Kriegsmarine, but nobody was paying attention to me. I was in my GI uniform, wearing a little wooly hat, wheeling that bike, and I was unobserved. When I got down to the baggage car, I knocked on the door and the clerk opened it. I handed him the bike. He gave me a receipt and slammed the door shut.

I took this opportunity to look around a bit. I saw a

stairway leading to the marshalling yard and for a moment thought: *Should I take off? Nobody is looking.* But then reality settled in. My high school German wasn't that good and I was in a U.S. uniform. *How would I survive?*

I walked back and gave the sergeant the receipt. He was eating a Wurst. He broke off a piece and handed it to me. "Danke," he said.

I responded, "Danke" and took the Wurst—my first food in three days.

He knew I wouldn't take off. My odds of survival weren't good out there.

There was a strange feeling we seemed to share with those Germans. There wasn't hatred between us. There was a feeling that the war was the real enemy, and we were both victims of it. That's the sense we had.

We got into the railroad car and traveled overnight to Fallingbostel. It was the location of Stalag XI-B—my new home.

TWENTY-SIX

We walked from the station up the hill into the entrance of the camp. Once through the gate, we entered the processing room. They took our pictures and gave us prisoner numbers. Mine was 201120. It was stamped onto a small wooden block, which I wore as a necklace. I kept it all these years. When things get tough, I look at it to remind myself of a time when things were worse.

The prison camp had different compounds. There were only about 250 Americans there when I first arrived, but there were also British, Canadians, New Zealanders, French, Belgian, Dutch, Greeks, Yugoslavs, Nigerians, Mongols, Azerbaijanis, sepoys, and many others. There were about twelve thousand prisoners in the camp. We were with the British. Some of the British had been captured at Dunkirk in the early part of the war in 1940. Some had been captured at Operation Market Garden in 1944.

The barracks was just one-story high, and we had three shelves between the floor and the ceiling. There were two men on the floor and two in each shelf—eight men stacked up in one column. You had to share a shelf with a buddy. My buddy was a fellow by the name of McGill. He played hockey for the Detroit Red Wings. He was a husky fellow and we were jammed in a shelf together.

We had half a blanket per man. Ours was grey-blue and written on it was "Pferde 1918." It was a horse blanket from the First World War.

Bedbugs and three kinds of lice infested the camp. During the day we did a lot of nitpicking, and at night the bedbugs and lice picked on us. Between the lice biting you and the cramped quarters, all you did was scratch and turn all night. For the two months I was in that place, I never had a decent night's rest.

The prison camp was a filthy place. There was no soap, no shaving cream, and no razor—just two faucets of cold water shared between 250 men. The latrine was about a hundred yards away and consisted of two concrete slabs with a couple of slits and a trickle of water underneath it.

The food was not gourmet. In the morning, we had a bowl—actually, a cup—of acorn broth. It was just like warm water. For lunch we had bread. It was dark, sour bread made from potato flour and edible cellulose (sawdust). It was one loaf for eight men. I had the little pen knife that I had hidden in my boot, so I was the bread cutter. I cut eight slices and the fellows would take them. But after a few days, a dispute emerged.

"His slice is bigger than mine!"

After a while, we came up with a way to settle it. We figured the solution was to give everyone a number. On Monday, number one had selection. On Tuesday, it was number two, and we went down the line. That ended the dispute with the bread.

For dinner we had a bowl of soup, and it was either turnip or sugar beet soup. When horses were killed in the vicinity, sometimes we would get a little horse meat. It was a low-calorie diet. I lost at least twenty pounds in two months. In the early part of the war, the British and some others in the camp worked on farms nearby, and they had more to eat. But things got worse as the war progressed.

Red Cross parcels were available. They came from Sweden to the port of Lübeck on the Baltic Sea. Then they were transported in "Red Cross" marked vehicles to the prison camps. The Germans, however, used Red Cross vehicles to transport munitions and war materials, and the Allied planes shot them up, so it was hard to get the parcels to the camps.

In the two months I was there, parcels arrived twice. We shared them, four men to a parcel: cheese, crackers, fruit bars, candy bars, and canned chicken. It was great; but when you ate that much on an empty stomach, it created digestive problems.

The first time we had a food parcel, I started having problems in the middle of the night. I figured I better head for the latrine. I climbed down the shelves, stepped over the people on the floor, and stumbled out the door. I got about halfway to the latrine before realizing I wasn't going to make it. I squatted. As soon as I did, the guard in the tower turned the searchlight on me. The guard in the next tower in line followed suit. The towers were about seventy yards apart, shining their two shafts of light, illuminating the effect of the parcel. I was like an actor on a stage, and my performance was symbolic of the distaste I had for the Third Reich. But, with dignity, I stood, pulled up my trousers, and walked back to the barracks. The two lights followed me all the way back.

TWENTY-SEVEN

For recreation we just walked around the compound like caged animals. One time we tried to play softball. We played about three innings until we ran out of energy and desire and just gave up. Most of the time, we sat around. There wasn't much talk of home or women or anything besides food and your empty stomach. Your whole existence centered on your empty stomach.

One time, I was on duty to pick up the soup. As I was heading over, I passed the Russian compound. I observed these pitiful Russians as the Germans wheeled in a cart of garbage. They dumped it in a pile, and I watched these poor wretches just fight over it.

Typhus had broken out before I arrived. It was spread by lice and many Russians died because they were not inoculated. Some of the fellows in the camp had festering wounds that weren't healing. When they got bad, they went to the infirmary. There were many amputations. Every day a burial cart was brought down the road next to our barracks. They had pine boxes with the national flag of the deceased on it.

We thought of escape. There were four barbed wires with concertina wire between them in the bank that surrounded the camp. To make a tunnel would have been impossible. We had no digging tools, no means of propping up the tunnel, and it was probably about 150 feet or more to the outside from the nearest point. Since the war seemed to be close to the end, we figured, why bother? However, there were two British fellows that attempted escape. They apparently killed a guard on their way out. They were caught two days later and executed.

We had roll call twice a day. Our guards were Herman the German and One-Eye Joe, two veterans from the Eastern Front. They lined us up in three ranks and counted us: drei, sechs, neun, zwölf, fünfzehn, (three, six, nine, twelve, fifteen) and so forth. They didn't really care whether we were all there. Some fellows were back in the barracks or in the latrine. But when they got to the end, they would always say, "Gut."

They didn't know any English, so as they went down the line, the guys would shout obscenities at them: "One-Eye's S.O.B.—You lousy kraut!" The Germans just ignored it. That was sort of the game we played every day.

One day during roll call, an American officer announced that FDR had died and Harry Truman was now president. We didn't even know who Harry Truman was. We weren't involved in the election. Later, I found out Harry Truman was a captain of artillery in the 35th Division during WWI.

As time went on, additional prisoners came into the camp, so we heard how the war was going. We knew when the Allies were across the Rhine and we knew they were advancing. Every day planes flew overhead and when they did, the Germans made us go into the barracks. I'm not sure why because certainly Allied planes weren't going to bomb the prison camp.

B-17s went over in the day. The sky was black with them. Several hours later they would come back the other way. Some were limping with their tails half-shot off and holes in their fuselage. Some crashed and the pilots were carried in as prisoners. At night, the British flew over in their Lancasters on their way to Berlin and other cities for bombing raids. We knew that the war was progressing, and sooner or later we hoped to be liberated.

One time a group was brought in for a couple of days from an Air Corp camp that had been overrun. They told us they had been in a road march and were forced to sleep in open fields in the cold. The stragglers were abandoned or shot. When they were told they were moving out again, we hid one of the guys in a trapdoor above our bunk for a while. Then I began cutting nine slices. The Germans didn't come in the barracks very often.

Each day the artillery outside the camp became louder, and our worst fear was being moved out of the camp in a road march. Three of us made a pact. We agreed that if we struggled out there, we would help each other, and if one fellow couldn't make it, we would carry him. Then rumors went around that we were to move out the next day.

That evening, we saw the red, white, and blue roundel of a British Spitfire come over the treetop and right over the camp. It waggled its wings and flew away. We knew that was a signal.

The next morning, we heard small arms fire, cannon fire, and two big explosions. The Germans blew up the water works and power station. The lights went out and the water stopped running. We heard firing in the woods.

The next thing we knew, two big British tanks came down the road: Cromwell and Churchill tanks. Painted on each vehicle was a little red rat—the British Seventh Armoured Division. They had been at El Alamein in Egypt. They chased Rommel across the desert from Tobruk to Benghazi to Tripoli, all the way to Tunis. They fought their way through Normandy, across northern France, Belgium, and into Germany.

The British had broken through the German line and set up a defense perimeter around camp. Pandemonium. Some had been prisoners for five years. Everybody cheered. Liberation day. It was one of the happiest days of my life.

T W E N T Y ˜ E I G H T

1945 MAY 4 AM 11 58
THE SECRETARY OF WAR DESIRES ME TO
INFORM YOU THAT YOUR SON PFC SCHOE-
LLER CRAIG A RETURNED TO MILITARY
CONTROL 20 APR 45
J A ULIO ADJUTANT GENERAL.

TWENTY-NINE

Even though we were freed, we didn't leave the camp at first because there were still German snipers in the woods. Later in the afternoon, we were able to exit through the fence. It was great to look back and see the camp from the outside. I saw some prisoners with a pig, carting it away, and a couple of Australians had some chickens.

We eventually made our way into a small general store. It was pretty well cleaned out except for candles. We picked up a big box of them and carried it back to the camp. Since we didn't have electricity, we lit them and set them up all around. Hundreds of candles burned brightly in our miserable surroundings. Men who had had little hope a few days before were now free and could think of home and seeing loved ones.

The emotion was released in song. Someone started singing "God Bless America" and hundreds of voices joined in. And it didn't stop there. There was a slight pause, someone thought of their favorite tune and the serenade continued. We sang "Home on the Range," "Amazing Grace," "The White Cliffs of Dover," "Don't Sit Under the Apple Tree," "Roll Me Over in the Clover," "Lili Marlene," and many more. It went on and on for hours until the candles gradually burned down, and weary but happy men fell off to sleep.

By that time, the room was stuffy. McGill and I decided to open the trapdoor above our bunk just to get a little fresh air. We were just about asleep when we felt rats crawling all over us. I thought: *How did rats survive without food in this place?*

THIRTY

1945 MAY 14 PM 10 44

THE CHIEF OF STAFF OF THE ARMY DIRECTS
ME TO INFORM YOU YOUR SON PRIVATE
FIRST CLASS CRAIG A SCHOELLER IS BEING
RETURNED TO THE UNITED STATES WITH-
IN THE NEAR FUTURE AND WILL BE GIV-
EN AN OPPORTUNITY TO COMMUNICATE
WITH YOU UPON ARRIVAL

J A ULIO THE ADJUTANT GENERAL.

THIRTY-ONE

The next day not much happened. We were waiting for the rest of the British Army to catch up. The following day, however, we got half a loaf of bread per man. We were deloused that night, and they put us on lorries in a convoy to go back to the airfield. We had fifty miles to go with about twenty lorries. Half of the convoy got lost in the darkness and went behind German lines, but somehow all the trucks arrived at the correct location the next morning—Diepholz.

We spent all day in Diepholz on the tarmac waiting for planes to come in and take us out. We became friendly with the RAF pilots. They were just young fellows, about eighteen or nineteen years of age. We told them about our experiences. They hopped in their Spitfires and took off, chased Germans, and then came back to tell us what they had done. Those RAF boys were great. We had a lot of fun with them. They saved England.

At the end of the day, we were the last plane out before dark. We flew out in a Dakota (a military version of the Douglas DC-3) and headed toward Brussels. Even though we had control of the sky, I kept looking out the window for Messerschmitts. But we made it back safely to Brussels under British control. That was the first time I ever flew in a plane.

When we arrived, we were deloused again, and I had my first shower, shave, and change of clothes in three months. What a wonderful feeling that was. I could have stood under that shower for days. They gave us clean uniforms with British berets and the equivalent of twenty-five dollars in Belgian francs. They said, "Fellows, just be back by tomorrow morning." With that, we jumped on the tram and away we went. We had ice cream and threw up. We had fish and chips and threw up. We had lamb stew and threw up. Nothing would stay down, but it sure was fun to eat again.

Then we went to a dance at the USO. I remember dancing with a Belgian girl. She couldn't understand what I was saying, and I couldn't understand what she was saying, but it was great to be back in civilization.

They gave us a big box of donuts. We went back to the barracks and distributed them among the other guys.

The next morning, we boarded box cars. We rode on the rails past the Waterloo battlefield, and I saw the pyramid with the British lion. We arrived in Namur and were under GI control. The war was in Allied hands.

Then we had the chance to send a wire home:

ALL WELL AND SAFE. BEST WISHES TO ALL AT HOME. LOVE CRAIG SCHOELLER.

THIRTY-TWO

From Namur, we went by train toward the coast. We went through the Somme Valley. We came through Picardy and Amiens and arrived at Saint-Valery, the location of Camp Lucky Strike—one of the many tent cities the U.S. Army had established and named after cigarettes.

There, we waited for transport back across the Atlantic. It was about a week before it arrived. When it did, we traveled to Le Havre and then took an LST (Landing Ship, Tank) to a ship in the outer harbor. We climbed up rope ladders to board.

Now for a bit of history. In April 1865, the Civil War had ended. The ex-prisoners of war from the Union wanted to leave the Confederate camps and return home. A paddle-wheel steamer, the *Sultana*, tied up at Vicksburg for repair, was to take these men up the Mississippi. The ship's capacity was only about four hundred passengers, but over two thousand ex-POWs boarded. The ship left after the boiler was fixed, and the men were excited to head home. All went well until just past Memphis when the boilers exploded, starting a fire on the ship. Most of the men could not swim but jumped into the water anyway. A few were saved, but most were lost. It was the worst maritime disaster in United States history with more deaths than the *Titanic*. The happiness of the war's end changed to grief. Eighty years later I almost experienced a similar tragedy while on board the troopship *George Washington*.

The *George Washington* left France with me and other ex-prisoners of war. It was originally a German ship but was confiscated by the U.S. in 1917. Woodrow Wilson went to the Paris Peace Conference on that ship. It was an old-timer, but we didn't care what we were on as long as it was heading home.

As we sailed across the English Channel, we were reminded that the war was still on. About halfway, a sub caught up with us. Luckily, we had destroyers with us, and they located it and dropped depth charges. I was on F Deck. Every time they dropped a depth charge, the plate next to my bunk vibrated.

We landed in Southampton, England, picked up wounded fellows, and started across the Atlantic toward the States.

The *George Washington* rode with a high center of gravity. Twice a day we were fed and the chow line was on the starboard side. When the chow line was in progress, the ship listed to one side. When it was done, the ship went back again. We listed twice a day all the way across the Atlantic.

Halfway across the ocean, the war in Europe ended. We were some of the first troops to arrive in New York after the war was over. Tugs pushed us to the same dock that I had left six months before. There were bands, balloons, and crowds of people cheering.

In all the excitement, everybody on board ran up to the deck. Naturally, the *George Washington* started to list. However, this time the listing was extreme. Sirens sounded and bells rang. My feet moved as fast as possible down the stairs. We rushed to clear the deck. Just in time, too. It could have been a tragic homecoming—to have had all that experience in Europe only to come back home and drown in the Hudson.

THIRTY-THREE

After that, ferry boats took us across the river to Hoboken, New Jersey, from where we rode a short distance to Camp Kilmer. The next day, we continued south to Fort Dix, New Jersey, and I was able to make a phone call to my parents. Several days later, I took a bus and a taxi and arrived home sweet home. My dad saw me first and gave me a big hug, and soon my mother joined us.

I was home for about thirty days and then reported to Asheville, North Carolina for reassignment. I was ordered to Fort Bragg, North Carolina and went into training for the invasion of Japan. I was scared. There were many U.S. casualties in the Pacific. Every farmer would be waiting for us with a pitchfork.

I also learned I would be in a 4.2 chemical mortar battalion, which was good news because I would not be on night patrols like I was in the infantry.

I took a train and a bus to Fort Bragg, and as I arrived at the camp, I heard all this excitement and commotion. Guys were jumping around and dancing. I asked someone, "What's going on?"

The fellow cheered, "The war is over! The war is over!"

President Truman had approved the use of atomic

weapons and we had dropped the bombs on Hiroshima and Nagasaki. The Japanese had surrendered, and the horrible war was over after six years.

I remember sitting down on some steps with my friend and giving thanks that we had survived.

THIRTY-FOUR

Aug. 14, 1945

Dear Mom + Pop:

I arrived here at camp just in time to hear the big news. Compared to the hysterical celebrations I hear over the radio, things here at Fort Bragg are rather quiet. Some of the fellows cheered and yelled a while, a few fired rifles, but most of us took the news happily and quietly.

There's a big mob down at the P.X. singing with great gusto but most of the fellows are standing around in small groups talking it over and speculating when they'll get home.

Once again I had a seat next to a sailor on the train. I guess I slept half of the way to Washington and arrived there at 8:00. I had to wait in the station until 9:30 and was hoping the news would come then. The whole place had that anxious, expectant air. I ate a sandwich, and they were swell, and then boarded the train. I was lucky. The coach was air conditioned and very clean. I slept most of the way down here, now and then taking a bite to eat. The train pulled in around 5:30 and I took a bus out to camp. I went down to the orderly room, turned in my furlough paper and then heard the news. Since then I've been listening to the radio. Right now Gabriel is blowing. He even sounds sad this night of nights.

As for me, I just can't realize it. I'm so happy I don't know

what to say. I can only thank God with all my heart.
 I'll write again tomorrow,
 Your son,
 Craig

T H I R T Y - F I V E

The shadow of war had been over me for a long time. The Japanese attacked Manchuria in 1931, and then the war in Europe started in 1939. As a school kid I wondered: *Am I ever going to war?* But a great weight was lifted off my shoulders, the clouds of war cleared, and now I could live a normal life.

I ended up getting a Master's in Mechanical Engineering at the University of Pennsylvania and went on to work for a company called Proctor & Schwartz, Inc. They made industrial equipment, heat processing equipment, and textile equipment. I worked in research engineering, design engineering, and sales engineering. I was there for thirty-five years, but I didn't use much that I had learned in the Army. Shooting a rifle or wielding a bayonet is not very useful in civilian life.

I worked hard in the Army and always gave my best. I went in a youth and came out a man. My final grade was Administrative NCO Staff Sergeant, in charge of a typing section at Fort Dix, New Jersey, which was the best break because I lived in Philadelphia and was home quite frequently. I handed out discharges until I finally left the Army in April of 1946.

I am proud of my service. When I look back on my experience in the Army, I have much to be thankful for. I grew up in a hurry and learned what is really important in life. I will always remember that when you wear the blue braid of the infantry on your cap, you can stand tall and look anyone in the eye. I had taken the difficult road and won.

Amen.

Epilogue

When I left the Army, I did not want to talk about my experience. I had no desire to go back to Europe. I had seen enough horror and desolation. I just wanted to forget about it all and get on with my life.

Fifty years had gone by, and the events of WWII were passing in history. But memories do come back. Like the Union and Confederate veterans that went back to Gettysburg in 1913, and the members of the Army Expeditionary Force that went back to Saint-Mihiel in 1968, veterans of the 35th Division returned to Europe in 1994.

There were forty of us and our wives in two buses. We spent two weeks traveling about twelve hundred miles across France, parts of Belgium, Holland, Germany, and Luxembourg.

We went to Normandy on D-Day plus fifty years and stayed in a motel in Saint-Lô. While we were sitting together, a woman entered with a brown bag in hand. She said she was looking for the veterans.

"Well, here we are," I responded.

With that, she revealed a bottle of Calvados—apple brandy. She told us that when the Germans overran her farm, they took everything but her apples, and this bottle of brandy was made from those apples. A fifty-year-old bottle of brandy. So, we toasted. We toasted the lady from Normandy and her farm. We toasted Normandy itself. We toasted the French, and we toasted our victory.[5]

In the morning, we attended a service on the beaches. We were at Utah Beach and then went over to Omaha. We had reserved seating and were moving into the grandstand as the dignitaries were filing in. There was Queen Elizabeth, François Mitterrand, Bill Clinton, and others. We could not see too well because some people were standing up and obstructing our view. I tapped the nearest man on the shoulder and said, "Would you fellows mind sitting down so we veterans can see?" When he turned around, I saw that it was Joe Biden! Looking down the line, I saw there was Specter, Glenn, Kerry, and about twenty other senators. They all sat down. That was the only time in my life I ever had that much influence. Now every time I see Joe Biden, I say, "Sit down, Joe."

When we were heading to Paris, I remember seeing a young girl with a sign in the front of her car that read "Thank you for my liberty."

We also spent time in a little town west of Nancy where one of the fellows was wounded. While we were looking around town, a woman approached us, and it turned out she was the mayor! She called her friends and they set up tables. We had wine, juice, and cheese. It was a friendly, little impromptu party.

---

[5] After speaking about this moment with my grandmother and his wife, Betty Lou Schoeller, she revealed that she did not like the taste of the brandy. Not wanting to hurt the woman's feelings, my grandmother hid her glass behind an object on a filing cabinet next to her seat.

Eventually, we went to Luxembourg City and then took a bus north to Boulaide. We came up the same hill that we had attacked fifty years ago. There wasn't any machine gun fire this time, but the whole town was there to welcome us. A little monument to the 35th Division had been constructed on the edge of town. The mayor and the dignitaries were there in their Sunday best with red, white, and blue ribbons. There was a band and color guard and the women, men, and children of the village all gathered around. The band played the Luxembourg national anthem along with "The Star-Spangled Banner."

The mayor came forward: "Welcome men of the 35th Division. We thank you for our freedom. We will never forget what you did for us, and we will tell our children and our grandchildren." Tears came to his eyes. Tears came to our eyes. We remembered how these people had suffered under Nazi rule and how we had paid an awful price for their freedom. The bugler played "Taps" while the kids of the town gave us long-stemmed red roses. We placed them on the monument.

After a while, we walked into the center of town. There were a few scars from bullets and shrapnel, but it looked very much like it did when I was in the war. As we strolled farther, the leader of our tour group came up to me and said, "Hey Craig, you were wounded near here. Why don't you give the speech today?" With that, he handed me a plaque.

It would have been nice if he had told me the night before. *What am I going to say to these people?*

We walked into a little hall. They had hors d'oeuvres, wine, lemonade, and orange juice. It was a pleasant reception. Then it was my turn.

I started by saying, "Mr. Mayor, citizens of Boulaide, fifty years ago I stayed in a house down the street. Behind the house was a church and on the church wall the Germans had written the following words: 'Heute gehört uns Deutschland, morgen die ganze Welt' (Today it is Germany that belongs to us, tomorrow it will be the whole world). How wrong they were. We drove them out of Boulaide, liberated the rest of Luxembourg, and won the war in the West. In memory of that time, I'd like to give you this plaque."

Also, in my pocket I had a little replica of the liberty bell. I handed it to the mayor and said, "I come from Philadelphia where my forefathers declared their independence and in view of our mutual love of liberty, I'd like you to take this little bell." He had a big smile on his face. That was a moment I'll never forget.

From that reception, we went over to a little inn where some women had prepared lunch for us. It was delightful food and a wonderful atmosphere. Everybody was gracious. We made friends with these people from Luxembourg.

After an hour or so, it was time to leave. We hopped on our buses and went up the same road that we had followed into the attack. We passed the spot where I had seen the dead German, passed the intersection where I could look down and see Baschleiden. Houses were rebuilt. We passed the farmhouse and the road intersection where we had seen the casualties. I saw the fields and those bitter woods.

I'm a real history buff and I've been to a lot of battle-fields from Saratoga to Yorktown and Antietam to Shiloh, but to be at a battlefield where you and your comrades struggled is an emotional experience. I was apprehensive.

It was springtime, so I didn't see the snow. I didn't see a Tiger tank or hear the clatter of machine guns or the roar of artillery. All I saw were the ghosts of brave, frightened young men. It was quiet. It was serene. The Ardennes was at peace. That was good to see.

Appendix B

Dear Mr. Schoetker,

My name is Wendy Maesen and I'm 26
years old. I live in Tegelen, this is 2 km
from Venlo. I got your address from Mr.
Wokkie.
I think you'll remember the Kaldenkerkerweg
in Venlo, this is a road on a small hill
you drove on 53 years ago. In a small
sideway from 'de kaldenkerkerweg' my
grandparents lived with their 6 children.
And thanks to you, and all the men from
the 35th Infantry Division they all survived.
After the war in 1945 my mother was
born. So indirectly we all thank our
live to you and all the great men who
came to Holland and fought for us.
My grandparents died at a very high age
and all my aunts and uncles are
still alive today (accept for one).
So what I'm trying to say is that you
have a special place in my heart and
I'll never forget what you did.
                    Love and a lot off
                    greetings from
                              wendy →
                              x x x

— 96 —

31-5-98

Dear Mr. Schoeller

My name is Wendy Maesen and I'm 26 years old. I live in Tegelen, this is 2 km from Venlo. I got your address from Mr. Wokke.

I think you'll remember the Kaldenkerkerweg in Venlo, this is a road on a small hill you drove on 53 years ago. In a small sideway from 'de Kaldenkerkerweg' my grandparents lived with their 6 children. And thanks to you, and all the men from the 35th Infantry Division they all survived. After the war in 1949 my mother was born. So indirectly we all thank our live to you and all the great men who came to Holland and fought for us. My grandparents died at a very high age and all my aunts and uncles are still alive today (accept for one). So what I'm trying to say is that you have a special place in my heart and I'll never forget what you did.

Love and a lot off greetings from

Wendy

xxx

Bibliography

134th Infantry Regiment Website. "320th Infantry Regiment Morning Report Index—Company F." Morning Report Index by Date. Accessed May 2, 2021. http://www.coulthart.com/134/mr-320-f-company/mr-320-index-f-company.htm.

Atpladmin. "Remembrance of Things Past: World War II Lecture Series at Abington Free Library." Abington Township Public Library. Last updated January 17, 2018. http://www.abingtonfreelibrary.org/remembrance-things-past-world-war-ii-lecture-series-abington-free-library.

Ballard, Ted. *Rhineland.* The U.S. Army Campaigns of World War II, CMH Pub 72-25. Washington, DC: Center of Military History, United States Army, 2019. https://history.army.mil/html/books/072/72-25/.

Cirillo, Roger. *Ardennes-Alsace.* The Campaigns of World War II, CMH Pub 72-26. Washington, DC: United States Army, Center of Military History, 2019. https://history.army.mil/html/books/072/72-26/.

Bibliography

Herrmann, Brian. "Exploring War and Translation: A Lost German Soldier's Letter Home." Capstone project. Susquehanna University, 2020. Endeavor. https://susqu-researchportal.esploro.exlibrisgroup. com/esploro/outputs/other/Exploring-War-and-Translation-A-Lost/991002248996405236?institution =01SUU_INST.

Kansas Adjutant General's Department. "35th Infantry Division." Accessed April 28, 2021. https://kansastag. gov/35thID_default.asp.

Roosevelt, Franklin. "'Day of Infamy' Speech." December 8, 1941. Joint Session of Congress, Washington, DC. Recording from the John G. Bradley Papers. National Archives and Records Administration, College Park, MD. MP3, 11 min. https://catalog.archives.gov/ id/1436350. Transcribed by Brian Herrmann, October 14, 2022.

Schoeller, Craig A. "The Ardennes Remembered." *World War II Lecture Series.* Presented by World War II Lecture Institute. January 28, 2004. DVD, 1 hr., 5 min. Personal copy.

Schoeller, Craig A. "Fighting Germans with 35th Infantry Div. 1945 Capture/Liberation." *World War II Lecture Series.* Presented by World War II Lecture Institute. Recorded February 16, 1999. Published January 1, 2004. DVD, 59 min. Personal copy.

Schoeller, Craig A. Interview. "Art of the American Soldier" Exhibit, National Constitution Center of Philadelphia. August 17, 2010. Video produced by Drexel University Goodwin College of Professional Studies. DVD, 49 min. Personal copy.

Schoeller, Craig A. Interview by John Holloran. La Salle University, June 24, 2009. Craig A. Schoeller Collection (AFC/2001/001/67745). Veterans History Project, American Folklife Center, Library of Congress, Washington, DC. https://memory.loc.gov/diglib/vhp/story/loc.natlib.afc2001001.67745/.

Schoeller, Craig A. Lecture. World War II Lecture Institute. Abington, Pennsylvania. Recorded December 19, 2000. Uploaded May 18, 2020. YouTube video, 1 hr 2 min. https://www.youtube.com/watch?v=RECLTCdTeJY.

Schoeller, Craig A. Lecture. *World War II Lecture Series*. Presented by Word War II Lecture Institute. May 2020. DVD, 1 hr., 21 min. Personal copy.

U.S. Army Divisions. "35th Infantry Division – Sante Fe." Accessed November 11, 2022. https://www.armydivs.com/35th-infantry-division.

Willmott, H.P., Robin Cross, and Charles Messenger. *World War II*. New York: Dorling Kindersley Limited, 2004.